T0064560

# DYING TO LIVE

# DYING TO LIVE

## A WOMAN'S CONSCIOUS
## JOURNEY THROUGH DIS-EASE

Malane Gargurevich

BALBOA.
PRESS
A DIVISION OF HAY HOUSE

Balboa Press books may be ordered through booksellers or by contacting:

Balboa Press
A Division of Hay House
1663 Liberty Drive
Bloomington, IN 47403
www.balboapress.com
1 (877) 407-4847

Because of the dynamic nature of the Internet, any web addresses or
links contained in this book may have changed since publication and
may no longer be valid. The views expressed in this work are solely those
of the author and do not necessarily reflect the views of the publisher,
and the publisher hereby disclaims any responsibility for them.

The author of this book does not dispense medical advice or prescribe the use
of any technique as a form of treatment for physical, emotional, or medical
problems without the advice of a physician, either directly or indirectly. The
intent of the author is only to offer information of a general nature to help
you in your quest for emotional and spiritual well-being. In the event you use
any of the information in this book for yourself, which is your constitutional
right, the author and the publisher assume no responsibility for your actions.

Any people depicted in stock imagery provided by Thinkstock are
models, and such images are being used for illustrative purposes only.
Certain stock imagery © Thinkstock.

Print information available on the last page.

ISBN: 978-1-5043-2923-1 (sc)
ISBN: 978-1-5043-2924-8 (e)

Balboa Press rev. date: 6/9/2015

**For My Beloved Father, Herbert A. Gargurevich**
May 17, 1941 – July 23, 2014

He was also known as Papa, Nono, Herberin, and Sargento (sergeant). You, my father, were my deepest joy, so close to my heart, always and in all ways in my heart. I felt frustrated with myself for taking so long with finishing this book. Although I thought I was finished a few months ago, my intuition kept telling me to wait before putting it out into the world (I wasn't sure why though).

Our human side, at times, gets frustrated instead of just trusting what is. Who knew that after five years of experiencing my own healing journey, now feeling well, vibrant, and blessed, that I would be putting these acquired practices or healing modalities to use for you?

I know that your spirit is being set free, and I was so blessed, honored, and privileged to be by your side for the last eight to nine weeks caring for you, along with my mother and sister. Thank you for that gift. It was a difficult journey. "Separating the caregiver and the daughter roles."

During this journey, I have seen, with my spiritual eyes and heart, the beauty of death. As one is passing or transitioning into the next phase of changing form, how beautiful it can be if we support our loved one. It is an act of selflessness. It's not about what we want for ourselves but about honoring what they need to make it easier for them. It's up to us to lovingly let go and let them know that it is okay. At times, we hold on so tightly that we confuse the individual passing. It keeps them stuck and they hold on longer, which interferes with their process. So let us honor those that we love, and always know that they are with us in all ways.

I spent much time singing or sharing mantras with my father. The mantra for transformation (which is listed below), in particular, was to assist his soul on its next journey. I lovingly stood by his side day by day, as my heart ached for this beautiful soul to let go. To share in this experience with him was one I would have never imagined. Even though I have had my own experiences of being in both worlds at the same time, to be in the presence of a loved one going through this transition was difficult. As he reached out to the Divine and communicated to many he had loved that had already crossed over, he was so welcomed and supported by the physical and non-physical world. I thank you, Eternal Father, for taking him with you to be by your side and to release him from the burdens he had held onto.

I would not have done this any other way with my father. I love you and bless you, as you have blessed me. May you fly to all of the glorious places your physical body always desired. I will miss you physically but look forward to having you in my field energetically. ¡Papito, te quiero mucho!

**Mahamrityunjaya Mantra** (maha-mrityun-jaya)
Om Tryambakam Yajamahe
Sugandhim Pushtivardhanam
Urvarukamiva Bandhanan
Mrityor Mukshiya Maamritat

# DEDICATION

I dedicate this book to my ancestors in present and past lives. I had my first major experience in nature while I was traveling in Peru, at the age of 16 years that forever changed me. I had one month of travel in this beautiful country and spent some time in Iquitos, Peru. During that time, Mother Earth and I merged as one. I watched eagerly as the indigenous people lived their lives in their villages, and I immersed myself completely in this way of being. Their desire to live as we do was non-existent, and it fascinated me.

Many years have passed since my Peru experience, which had eventually landed me to my next destination. I had the amazing opportunity to live in the mountains on the Hawaiian Island of Molokai for almost six years. At this time of my life, it became pivotal on how much time I wanted or desired to spend outside tending to the needs of the earth, as it assisted me in my own transitions. It has been well over twenty years since I realized that, for me, nature was the ultimate healer.

I dedicate this book, this tool, to all of the amazing beings and animals that befriended me and taught me so much. To the Barn Owl that found me on Molokai and continued to visit me for five years after he allowed me the opportunity to help heal him after his injury. To my parents, who did not always understand my way of being, but now do. Without you, this would not have been possible in this lifetime. To my sisters, who have always presented me with some sort of information, be it astrological, esoterical, or a form of divine guidance. To Mother Nature who never ceases to surprise me. I walk lightly upon the earth as to not impose upon her graciousness. You have blessed me many times. And lastly, to my daughters, you beautiful old souls that continue to inspire me with the words of wisdom that so delicately and kindly roll off your tongue. I also express my gratitude to the divine guidance that has assisted me and continuously inspires me to this day and allows me to inspire others, as my vehicle serves as a conduit.

# Acknowledgements

I would like to acknowledge Dave, a psychic holistic pharmacist. You were a dear friend and an amazing being. Your intuitive guidance, when I needed assistance in my healing, was literally lifesaving. Your insights and wisdom, plus your demeanor, are truly missed. May your soul be peaceful, and shall our paths cross again in another lifetime.

To the late Dr. Ann Wigmore, whose knowledge, dedication, and perseverance with the Raw Living Foods movement has inspired many. I first read your book in my 20th year of life not knowing I would be putting it into practice so many years later. There are countless trays of sprouts, wheatgrass, and many raw foods that reside in my kitchen so lovingly, for many to enjoy.

I would like to acknowledge my sister, Michelle Gargurevich, for all of her time of editing, spiritual advising, and just being a friend. You have been a true asset to me in so many ways.

# PROLOGUE

I would like you to know who I am, or, who I really was. I was born in Queens, New York, on July 21 of 1969. I do not really remember my life in this urban environment at all, as far as living there myself. I was the second-born child of my parents. They were originally from different locations in South America. English was my second language. By my third year of life, my parents moved us to the suburbs of Long Island, NY. Growing up in the suburbs in the early to mid seventies was sometimes a challenge, as we were the only Spanish-speaking family in the neighborhood at that time, which I was often made fun of for. I was the middle child of two other sisters. I have twin older brothers as well (they are the oldest out of all my siblings), but sadly, we did not grow up together. Though now, we are very well involved, which is beautiful.

I did still spend a lot of time in Queens, NY, as my beloved grandmother (my maternal grandmother) resided there. I was very involved with her, which was always quite interesting. She only spoke Spanish and came to America later in her life, possibly around her sixtieth year of life. She was quiet and magical, and that fascinated me. What I did not know at the time was that she was a healer. She had been gifted with healing abilities that came to her naturally. She often had many people in her home or was traveling to New

York City to do healings or attend healings at churches and such. It never really dawned on me what she was doing. She was just my grandmother, and I was young. I just always remembered that when I would see her, she had a nice lunch prepared. Then she would sit me on the couch and place her hand on my head, and I would wake up hours later. I always awoke refreshed and not knowing what had happened thinking to myself, "She did it again!"

From what I could remember, I was always prepared for anything. Even on my younger journeys, going back to my fifth year of life, I always had a hat, gloves, and a scarf ready. It did not matter the season. What mattered was that I was going somewhere, and I was ready. My mother appreciated this aspect of me. She told me she never had to ask me to get prepared because, well, I always was.

I always remember feeling very loved. My relatives adored me and some of my parent's friends did as well. They seemed to go out of the way for me at times. Other traits about me are that I was outgoing yet introverted, a very stubborn child and yet completely loving. But my parents never said anything about this. It was my own realization. I was stuck with my beliefs no matter what. Not finding the flexibility that could have balanced things out, I followed these patterns, as my father did. I was not a spoiled child nor were any of my siblings. I do remember, however, that when it was my older sister's birthday, and she received her birthday gift, apparently so did I, even though my birthday was two months later. This happened for a few years. I don't think my sister always appreciated that.

You could say I was the classic "tom boy," as I much preferred being outside collecting bugs and getting dirty. I would spend as much time outside as possible and was quite adventurous. Most of my time as a child was spent rescuing animals of all sorts, such as rodents, birds, and the many cats that lived outdoors. I adored and lovingly gave them all of my attention. Although this was not always appreciated by my parents, this was who I was. You are probably asking, "Why does any of this really matter? What does it have to do with this book?" I believe that part of it was my strong communion with nature, which includes animals. This is part of my calling and union with God. Besides, I would like you to get to know me from the beginning. A big part of my childhood, along with rescuing animals, was that I had the ability to see spirits. I often had deceased relatives visit me as a child, but at that time, I was fearful because I did not understand.

As you learn about me, and I reflect upon my younger years, you will notice as much involvement as I had in nature, there was still an imbalance within me. I was very shy and quiet, labeled the "good girl" because I never complained or rebelled. On the inside I wanted to say what was on my mind but could not get myself to do it when something bothered me, when I was in disagreement, or even just wanted to voice my opinion.

I remember vividly when my aunt was visiting to attend my grandmother's funeral that during our time together in the car, she said, "Good little girls don't talk" and "Good little girls don't ask questions." I thought to myself, "That is interesting." Also, later in the day while eating food and playing, she said something to the effect of "Good little girls sit down." Okay, "I will try," I thought.

We allow behaviors to mold us, even if it does not feel right. We do not acknowledge our inner knowing so many times. This became my pattern. This was an unhealthy habit that did not serve me well. I carried this pattern until my early twenties. At that time, I had a realization. It took me many years to finally notice that it was not making me feel good. What I mean is, I knew for a long time that it did not make me feel good, but that day I thought, "I do not want to do this anymore. I am done. Let me change this NOW!" Although my demeanor is for the most part peaceful, I had all these repressed emotions stored inside my mind. There was nowhere for them to go. And with that being said, they manifested into unhealthy vibrations or intentions in my skull. Thoughts are things. These things grow and can produce healthy vibrant cells or mutated organisms within ourselves.

From a metaphysical standpoint, it made sense for me to have this condition in my brain. I had to learn how to re-boot or re-program my thought forms in a way that served me well. There were years upon years worth of negative emotions that I had stored in my computer (brain) that had nowhere to go. They were never released. There was no defragmentation process, no clean up. So what were they to do? They grew and manifested into illness. Mutated micro-organisms took over like a virus in a computer. Some are easier to clean up, and others can be very aggressive and destructive. A book by Louise Hay, "Heal Your Body," has such pertinent information. Everybody should have this book in their library. If you look under brain, this is what you will find. *Brain: Represents the computer, the switchboard. Tumor: Incorrect computerized beliefs. Stubborn: Refusing to change old patterns.* I manifested this all by myself with my thought forms. Obviously not intentionally, but I caused this.

So maybe being the "good girl" was not really the best thing. We often think that we inherit conditions, disease, or illness genetically. I am not claiming that a condition, disease, or illness cannot be inherited or be a genetic factor. I am simply stating this through my personal observation that more often than not, we inherit thinking patterns, which can create those conditions or illnesses that were carried in our families. Here is some food for thought: We as a human race have many recipes that are passed down from generation to generation. It always stays the same, we never change it. What if you want to change it and enhance it in some way? Maybe you adjust the measurements or add different ingredients or remove some. The same can be addressed for illness. Look at the possibilities. If I had expressed my thoughts lovingly, instead of "being in my head," to others when I may have been angry, sad, confused, or whatever the emotion was, it would have been released. My brain would not have developed a disharmonious state. We can change this through our thought-form process. It can be such an amazing process.

I was not the child that complained about ever having headaches, nor did I as an adolescent or adult. I remember prior to finding out about my condition, which was an aggressive form of brain cancer that usually takes you within a few months, that I had an experience, which to say the least was quite unpleasant and frightening. I was driving on the highway one day just doing errands, and out of nowhere, this horrible pain on the back side of my head came. I thought I was going to black out and had to stop driving. This pain occurred many times after this initial time. The pain level was high and unbearable, always in the same spot (back left hand side). This is the cerebellum, which is deep in the core of the brain. I learned a lot about the brain during this time, and how each area and location releases particular hormones and controls parts of the body. It really is an amazing organ. I noticed at times that my speech was unclear. I began to slur my words and became tongue twisted often. It was embarrassing for me. This seemed to happen during times of inflammation. Another symptom that I experienced was an uncomfortable feeling in my eyes, mostly on the left side. They hurt a lot, and the light aggravated me intensely. This was due to the pressure on the ocular nerves. I was constantly squinting me eyes because my vision became blurry. It was suggested by one doctor I have my eyes examined, which I did. After many tests and time that could have been utilized elsewhere, I came out with perfect vision, as per the optometrist. Doctors seemed to have a hard time listening to me when I was explaining my circumstances. The pressure and discomfort was not because I needed glasses or because I reached a point in my life when our vision changes, but from all the pressure.

I actually stopped all night driving for one year because it was hard for me to see well and adjust to headlights. Plus the fact that I became very forgetful and always got lost gave me more of a reason why I shouldn't drive at night.

After these experiences, that is when I was scheduled for my first MRI. At that point, I had several reputable doctors read my reports. Then I read the report many times and just looked at it. I was in shock! What was I going to do? Who was going to take care of my children? The doctors and I discussed what actions to take and narrowed them down. From this point on, after officially being diagnosed with Brain Cancer, I changed my life completely. I was already eating healthy nourishing foods and practicing different healing modalities, but I took it to a whole new level.

I went from a healthy vegetarian-based diet to strictly Raw Living Foods (thank you, Ann Wigmore). As soon as my children left for school, I spent one hour in meditation. The regimented routine I integrated into my lifestyle was life changing and saving, to say the least. We all know routines can get boring. You just take it day by day, and play with it. Nothing is ever written in stone. This is how my day started:

5:45 am - 2 ounces of wheatgrass

6:30 am - wake kids up for school

7:00 am - have a cup of tea with children during breakfast

7:15 am - kids leave - I drink 12 ounces of fresh vegetable juice

7:30 am - 1 hour of meditation with divine intuitive guidance

8:30 am - 1 hour of energy healing on myself

9:30 am - 2-hour nap or relaxation

12:00 pm - prepare raw meal

2:00 pm - read an educational book on different healing modalities (knowledge is power)

3:30 pm - get acclimated to children coming home from school

4:00 pm - I prepare 12 ounces of fresh vegetable juice for self and children

5:00 pm - Next 2 hours are spent doing chores and/or family activities and dinner

7:00 pm - 2 ounces of wheatgrass

8:30 pm - Meditation then off to sleep

This is how I spent much of my time for a few years. During the warmer months of the year, I spent as much time outdoors as I could to receive the healing energy of the sunlight and absorb Vitamin D. I did participate with my "routine" in the forest or by the ocean whenever it was possible. The healing effects are magnified when we submerge ourselves in these types of environments. Ionic charges assist in restoring us as we are near the ocean. This is why many enjoy the ocean so much. The vibrations from plants and trees in the forests are so loving and warm.

I did learn some time later in my healing journey that my maternal grandfather, whom I never had the opportunity to really know, left this earth due to a health challenge as well. In fact, he also had brain cancer. It was surgically removed, but then the cancer relocated into another organ. He died shortly thereafter. Apparently his sister died of the same condition. As I discuss later in this book, many times you hear one say, "I inherited this disease" or "It is genetic." I do not doubt that that is possible, however, what I am trying to express is that even though I did not get to know my grandfather and his sister, perhaps we shared the same thought forms or habits. Or perhaps I had a lack of positive thought forms and had some kind of energetic imprint absorbed while in utero, as I was in his presence, that may have not allowed me to be more expressive and get "out of my head." There are many possibilities.

I'm not exactly sure what my relatives whom I mentioned earlier who also had tumors in the same area had experienced, but I surely can tell you what I did, aside from what I told you earlier. Fatigue and sleep deprivation were a regular part of my life at this time. It was very hard to sleep with this constant pain. The left lower part of my backside felt so bruised, along with tingling sensations and stabbing pains. I would place ice packs on my pillow and lay my head on the packs to decrease the inflammation, which meant "less pain." Basically I was numbing myself to alleviate the pain.

# INTRODUCTION

I write this today to bring to the attention of all beings that for every thought that crosses our mind is a manifestation, whether it is a positive or negative influence. Our actions cause reactions. We may also come into this lifetime with many things to work through from past lives.

When illness or disease sets in, let it be a time where it can teach you more about yourself. It is usually an opportunity to see what we need to change in our lives – to address what is not resonating within us. Our illness or disease can be a repercussion of thought forms from while we were in utero or even from past lives or how we are currently living. So the key is to look into the self deeply. There are so many wonderful holistic energy workers all over the world to assist. Better yet, why not study these modalities yourself so you can learn and help align your body emotionally, mentally, physically and or spiritually. Even if it is just for you, that is okay. We can learn these modalities, and some of us are just born with these natural gifts to assist ourselves, our families, or others.

When illness came into my life, it was a great teacher. I would say it was my greatest teacher. It has taught me well and continues to do so. It allowed me to become more congruent with myself, to align and tune in, if you will.

This divine guidance gave me the opportunity to start fresh when I was advised I had a very short amount of time left. With the divine spirit, it gave me the faith and strength to move forward and did not allow me to lose sight when I heard some of the information that was presented to me by doctors. "What do you mean I have three to six months? This cannot be possible." I was told during meditation to keep my emotions in balance, otherwise disharmony would occur. This can be a very emotional time, but the assistance given was truly a blessing and continues to be.

I send much love to all of you, whether you have a health challenge or not. Love is a beautiful gift. I wish unconditional love to all of you. My love for myself is true, and my love for all of you is true. Be true to yourselves, and honor who you are. We need not compromise. Do what feels right to you, and listen to yourself.

A very important lesson that I learned along my journey is that we are all so unique and different from one another. We all have different intentions, and we should be aware of others, as well as our own. As for every action, there is a reaction. Somebody else's intentions to help you may not always be in your best interest, although it may appear that way.

As we assist each other in the process of life for whatever it may be, it is important to leave and remove all ego. With ego, there cannot be love. To assist one another, it must simply be an unconditional self-less act. Love is always the answer. With love, all things grow and flourish.

So please be mindful and aware of unspoken words, as every interaction that takes place with others may have repercussions. Be fully present and with clarity. Ask yourself, "Is this for my highest good?" There are many things that take place in a dualistic world. Some things that cannot be physically seen or touched. Some of us are aware, and some of us choose not to be, but nonetheless, we are not the only beings that exist. And with that being said, non-physical contracts can be in effect, although we may not know it at the time or even know what they are. But they do exist. With these contracts, we may be bound to others in a way that may not serve us well just as psychic cords bind us to something or someone.

Many actions or deeds that may have taken place in a past life may have to do with a discomfort or learning lesson in this present life. Karma is a very interesting fact in many, if not all, of our life lessons or experiences. Everything happens for a reason. There is no judgment. So as one is in the process of a healing journey or a journey, nonetheless, let us look into our past so we can find out why we created this situation for ourselves in the present and clear it up for our future. Now wouldn't that be a fascinating act to take place? We can adjust our lives so we are able to live in our bodies more harmoniously on an emotional, mental, physical, and spiritual level. Let us clear all the debris that holds us back and continue to move forward and achieve emotional freedom and liberation.

This journey was a difficult one, but the courage, faith and strength that it provided me into this present time was truly a gift. I am thankful for all that I have learned. The pain and suffering transformed me into a lighter being. I had two choices. One way was to allow myself to succumb to it and be in a continuous disharmonious state until I was no more, or the second way was to surrender and let go. Once I surrendered, everything was alright. I was not in a resistive state anymore, which could not allow anything positive to flourish. Do you understand? Our thoughts, feelings, and beliefs plant seeds. What are your intentions? Let us plant a seed that will serve us well.

Please enjoy the many modalities, books, and other tools so readily available to us. They will make such a positive change in your life. Study and learn. Expand your mind and allow. I would also like to add that the information presented in this book is not intended to diagnose, treat, cure, or prevent any illness or disease. It is merely a tool that was divinely guided and lovingly prepared to assist any individual on their healing journey called Life. Be well and be blessed.

For starters, what I would like to say to you is, "Welcome to my journey." It is one that started a particular way and ended completely different from what one may expect. When one decides to make such a decision of being on a spiritual quest or healing journey, much shifting occurs. I was truly blessed with all of these amazing gifts that the universe provided to me during this transition in my life. Many individuals came and went. Some individuals stayed and continue to do so. But, nonetheless, I am grateful to all, as all were masterfully put there for a reason. As I reflect upon all of the experiences that happened with physical and non-physical beings, one thing I have to say is, "Thank You." I truly was supported by so many angels.

I invite you to acknowledge your feelings during this reading, as it is part of the healing process. Allow this to be of inspiration, whether you are on a healing journey or not. But truly, we all are in one way, shape, or form. Are we not? May we all be well. Every single one of us.

I made the decision of leaving my home and family for thirty days. For me to make such a drastic decision was enormous. I vacillated with this for some time, but with divine guidance, I was off on my Journey. I hope you enjoy all of the creations that transpired during this quest, whether poetry, recipes or other things of creation.

Before we go into my thirty-day journey, I share with you much of my most intimate moments with myself and with the divine intuitive guidance that had always presented itself to me. I sit here for hours remembering the moments, days, months, and years of how my life used to be. I never thought I would be in this position. Every day is an opportunity for growth though. Every moment must be appreciated to reflect upon the gifts that are presented to us daily. We are so blessed and should acknowledge all that comes our way. That includes all things - the good, the bad and the ugly. Everything happens for a reason. So as I sit here, I learn more about myself, which helps me and in turn, assists in helping you. I was on a mission of whatever time I had left here to help you. It appears I am still here.

There are those that may or may not understand what I am about to say. And that is, "To be in the light is "THE WAY." I have had my experiences of crossing several times with one foot on the ground and one hand towards the heavens. This is a very beautiful process one should not fear. The process of leaving the body is not death but simply changing form. We humans sometimes do not understand, and we feel the sadness that occurs within ourselves because we form attachments to individuals or material objects. We miss them and understandably so. There is no judgment, as we all grieve differently, and there is no time frame on how long it takes. The loss of a loved one doesn't necessarily mean they will never be with you though. We still can have the communication we desire with one that has passed, if we open up the channels. The channels must be clear at all times, releasing emotional and mental residue that does not serve us. We all have the potential of such things.

To begin this process, I head to California. I wanted to share with you some of the amazing things that I or we did. Of course, everyday was completely different from the rest, and everywhere I went was a new adventure. Each place welcomed me with love, sunshine, inspiration, and encouragement.

# DAY #1 - MAY 10, 2010

This morning, I started out at 6:00 am for my flight to California to begin my 30-day journey to recovery. I was a bit tired being that I had to leave the house at 4:00 am to get to the airport and allow time for all of the checkpoints and all of the good stuff that comes along with traveling these days. Don't forget to put the 1-2 ounce liquid bottles in a Ziploc. We've all lost items by not doing that, right? Anyway, so I arrived in California at about 1:00 pm.

I had an amazing burrito near where we were staying. Then we arrived at a friend's home, and I took a long nap – four hours to be exact! I felt much better. The rest of the evening was catching up with new friends and unpacking and settling in. It was comforting to be in a place where I was only responsible for myself and did not have to worry about taking care of children or pets.

I pick up the pieces of my soul as
they sprawl across the streets
For another spirit lifted me to an unknown familiar place
I hear you as the wind passes through the darkened
evening to collect any misinterpreted thoughts
Tomorrow I will be whole
Voices carry, laughter, smiles, energy, healing
I am here longing for knowledge

# Day #2 - May 11, 2010

I woke up around 7:30 am, and I felt refreshed, which was a pleasure and very unusual these days. For the last nine months, I often felt zombie like. This morning, I was awoken with the glorious sounds of many different birds. As I usually did, I would prepare a green smoothie for breakfast (always trying to keep the cells happy) and sat in the backyard dining area. The sun warmed my skin and soothed my heart. It was pleasant to feel the temperature increasing as the day went by. Today, I pretty much sunbathed and took advantage of the weather. I was a little sleepy as the day went by due to the time difference, but it was working more for me than against me.

> A newly opened leaf reaching towards
> the sun for its very first time
> Growing with every drop of dew
> Planting itself deeper into the earth

# DAY #3 - MAY 12, 2010

Today is my older sister's birthday who happens to be my best friend. I gave her a call as soon as I woke up. I usually never miss a day without speaking to her. It seems kind of weird when I do. As I did yesterday, most of my day was spent sunbathing out in the back, as I knew the next three days we would be out all day exploring and sightseeing. I woke up again feeling rested and refreshed. I found myself looking in the mirror noticing the changes with my skin. It was amazing to see, in just a few days, how much the peace and quiet has helped me. For such a long time, I could not recognize myself anymore. I had such dark circles under my eyes and dehydrated skin. It was nice going to sleep early and waking and seeing me, as I used to be.

Cleanse away the darkness
Bring me to the light
Healing hands
Divinity, I give myself to you

# DAY #4 - MAY 13, 2010

We are going out today at about 12:00 noon until around 11:00 pm tonight. I figured I should rest a bit today and not go out so early because I would have a very active day. But I feel AWESOME. The temperature here depends on what area of California you are in. It's about 65 degrees in the morning. Then by 10 or 11 am, it gets up to 85 degrees. At night, it's a bit cooler, like 70 degrees. I had an awesome breakfast again, and for all who know me, well, yes, I packed a lot of delicious raw healthy snacks for the road. There is one thing that most people who know me well know, and that is that I always travel with food as to avoid being irritable. We head out to San Francisco to Fisherman's Wharf and ended up at Pier 39, which was way COOL! After we parked, we walked into the pier area, which had every kind of food available (except RAW). My senses where aroused by all of the different aromas at the same time. I really enjoyed seeing a young musician that was playing in the crowds. He was a cross between Bob Dylan and Johnny Cash. He actually had a drum set attached to his back with strings attached to hands and feet, like a marionette, to strike the drum when he needed to. Along with that, he was playing a guitar, singing, and playing a harmonica, of course. He was amazing! From there on, we walked into a coffee shop and headed down the pier. My companion asked me to go through those doors and make a right. I asked why, and he said, "Just go. You will figure it out." And to my surprise, there were groups of sea lions resting on floats in the water by the pier. Apparently, this group has been coming here for many years. They were a noisy bunch and full of happiness, as they basked their leathery skin while the paparazzi looked on. I was so enthralled with them, as I have only seen them on television. Adjacent to where the sea lions were resting was Alcatraz. I have to say, from afar, Alcatraz looked beautiful, but I am sure happy I never lived there. After spending some time at Pier 39, we headed over to the Golden Gate Bridge, which I expected to be Gold but was Red instead. It was the most beautiful bridge I have ever seen. We went to the observatory area and took some pictures doing the tourist thing. We did not stay that long, as it was quite chilly. I was glad that I was prepared for that. The fun really started when we drove to Fort Kronkite, an old military base. The purpose of this destination was that you can go hiking there. Honestly, I was terrified, since I had not been that active since my last relapse with brain cancer in late March of this year. Of course, I was up for a challenge. I do want to tell you that I am feeling FABULOUS though. It's the best I have felt in a really long time. As an added bonus, I got to see a beautiful hummingbird. So now I was being put to the test. My companion said that he would always take people there who where rehabilitating from an illness to gauge how they were doing. I will tell you that I was a bit concerned. It was in total about a 6- mile hike. The first three miles where straight up a mountain, but wow, I never felt so invigorated, and it was so awesome! I was told that of all the people he had taken there, I was the only one that didn't complain and made it all the way. I was really proud of myself. There were some caves, and it was surrounded by the Pacific Ocean with hawks and vultures everywhere. I was so happy, I wanted to cry. After Fort Kronkite, we went through this beautiful city called Sausalito, which was kind of like Port Jefferson, New York, but even nicer with the most beautiful flowers and docks.

Live like it's your last day
Live like it's your last day
Open your soul to the holy light

# Day #5 - May 14, 2010

We started out at about 9:30 am and were out until 10:45 pm. It was a long day! I covered a lot of ground today. There was much traveling and sightseeing. I am not familiar with this area of California, only Los Angeles. Even though it was a very long day, I was amazed by so much of the beauty that I saw. I started heading towards Walnut Creek. The road trip to get to there was wonderful because it was all countryside and mountains. There were so many beautiful horses, cows, and sheep along the way. Finally, I arrive at Walnut Creek. The city had a very upscale kind of vibe happening. People, in general, seemed quite happy and pleased with life. And, really, there are many reasons why we should be. Every day is truly a blessing.

I ended up having an unexpected late lunch at this really great restaurant that we do not have on the east coast. OKAY, moving on, so we end up at P.F. Chang's, and I said, "Wow, that smells AWESOME." The interesting thing is that my party and I had dinner reservations there at 6:00 pm, and when we passed the restaurant, it was about 4:00 pm. We noticed a sign that said $3 - $6 from 3:00 – 6:00 pm and decided to eat early - taking advantage of happy hour, which was all food and some drinks. As my daughters would say, "SCORE!!!!!!" So we ended up in total ordering six ENTREES. They were so good- two vegetable dumplings, two chicken stir fry in lettuce wraps, one Mongolian order of Ribs, and lastly, an order of seared Ahi Tuna. All I could say is, "OH MY GOD!! My dress became very, very tight, but afterwards, we had time to walk around and time for me to return to my regular self instead of feeling like I was in my first trimester of pregnancy. I did have two drinks, believe it or not - PEAR MOJITOS – "LOVE IT!!!" They were quenching, soothing, and comforting at the same time, like a cool breeze on a hot summer day! So basically, it was pear mojitos and sake (Japanese rice wine) and a BEER, oh my! As it turned out, we cancelled our dinner reservations and enjoyed many dishes, as you can see, for what it would have cost for only two meals at dinner, without the specials. It was finally time to head over to the BALLET, so we walked our glutinous selves over there. I prayed for a BOWEL MOVEMENT of some sort. Yes, I really did go there. As we finally made our way to the theatre, I sat there feeling sausage like and AMAZED at the same time watching these men and women in tights and colorful outfits. It was not your typical performance. It was contemporary, which means all and any styles. There were three different acts. My favorite was the second act. It was a compilation of intense percussion music using glass bottles and paper. I am a woman who loves percussion. Drumming is a passion that resonates within my soul. Drum, dance, get your soul moving, and free yourself. Do it as much as possible. So as you can see, I had a very exciting, and entertaining day.

## Mirrors

Our spirit lurks with unknown shadows
Dancing with the forbidden to escape truth
Every ounce of fear inhibits our being
All mirrors are hidden
The common man hides within himself
He hides beneath the words he longs to speak
Beneath the pounding of his chest
Behind the mask waiting
Looking for answers he's been carrying
We are the resource, the light, the truth
Beneath the layers of poison a radiant Being exposed
Unfold, shed your skin, and see the reflection
that you've been hiding from

# Day #6 - May 15, 2010

NOW, let us get to Saturday. Is everybody still here? This was a lot of fun. I went for a drive along the Sacramento Delta River, which is surrounded by so many old bridges (remember Bridges of Madison County) and wind mill farms (go GREEN POWER). As we got onto the FREEWAY (as they say in CA because they barely have any tolls unlike New York), my companion eventually turned into some industrial-looking area, and I wondered what we were doing there. We ended up pulling into the "JELLY BELLY" Factory where they make their famous jelly beans, along with other candies (for the sugar connoisseurs). Apparently, at some point, I mentioned something about the jelly bean factory, and I said I wanted to go. I don't remember exactly when I had said that. I must have been having a brain freeze or something. So here I was at Jelly Belly. My inner child and I were so happy and had a great time. We went on our tour and had to wear Jelly Belly hats, which I brought home. They showed us all of the steps and processes that it takes to make a JELLY BEAN. They make about 30,000,000 a day. Can you believe that? Nice business, it seems, to be working for them. Anyway, throughout the tour, they let you taste different jelly beans, as they went through each step. When the tour was over, you could go into their store, and they had an open bar (not the kind you are thinking of). It was an open bar with tons of different jelly beans, and you could sample whichever you wanted, as many times as you wanted for free. Sorry girls. You missed this one! I decided to stop after about 7 to 10 different samples (didn't want to go into a sugar rush). I definitely left happily and smiling like a 4-year old.

From there on, the next destination was Napa Valley, capital of wine country or wine universe. We stopped for our first wine tour and decided to skip the "official" tour and the price but sort of did the tour on our own. We went into the wine cellars, took some pictures, and left quickly, as to not get into trouble. Their grounds were beautiful, luscious, and aromatic. Now, onto the big guns. We stopped over at Sterling Winery and officially paid for a tour on their grounds that were self guided and included wine tasting and a gondola ride (like a cable car with style) up and down the mountain. We headed up the mountain in the gondola and took some pictures from the sky ride. For our first tasting (I am not much of a wine drinker, although I do enjoy Maurizio's parents' wine tremendously – Maurizio is my brother-in-law who comes from Italy, and his family has vineyards in their yard), we have a white wine. I struggled a bit, but amazingly enough, I finished it, as we were at our own leisure on the tour, educating ourselves on wine mastery. On to taste test #2 (by the way, the wines got better as we went along, and so did the scenery). By this time, we were watching monitors showing us how to do the pressing and all (not the way that Lucy Ricardo did it either) and joyfully walking and occasionally skipping through the walk area to find ourselves heading to our third tasting. This was my favorite wine, and the scenery here was on a rooftop overlooking lush mountains with hawks flying by mystically. This was a beautiful container garden on a rooftop patio. With all walks of life and many tongues of language spoken here, it was a most interesting place to people watch. To our amazement, we realized that the person who poured the wine now changed shifts, so we decided to have a second pour (I mean why not - we were already here). Sangiovese was the one we actually had sampled four times (they only fill the glass ¼ of the way - please do not worry, as I can assure you this happens every 40 years with me). Yes, the wine pourers actually changed so many times that we decided to give it a whirl not just for the wine but also for the poetic history from every wine pourer, as they expressed it so fluently and romantically. This was the place to be. After a few ¼ glasses and full sun for at least three hours, it was now time to move onto wine taste #4. Off we went from the rooftop patio and through this dimly lit indoor walkway leading outside and up several flights of floral stairways taking us into a quaint dining area, or another outdoor patio, with beautiful large white umbrellas. I call this the "shaded patio" with the most glorious view of redwood trees that seem as if they would reach into the heavens. It was breathtaking and life sustaining. Just so you know, we did not have to go too far for taste #5 because it was in the same location as taste #4. We didn't spend that much time up there due to the fact that we spent so many hours on the first patio, but it was glorious! We actually were able to keep our wine glasses from Sterling Winery as a souvenir. We should have only had 2 but somehow, ended up with half a dozen. Not bad! We have a nice little collection now. Unfortunately, it was getting close to closing time, and down we went in the gondola that we had to share with others. It was a tight squeeze, but we did it and had much conversation with a couple from Oregon.

I know this has been a long day, but I felt wonderful and was loving life. It was now about 6:00 pm, and we were off to find something to eat. I did forget to mention that at the first winery, we had some lunch that I packed for us. Of course I made a delicious organic salad blend with an array of vegetables, along with trail mix and with some carrot and celery sticks. I do try to stay as close as possible to my typical eating patterns, as it sustains my life. So back to dinner, we drove into some city called Yountville that reminded me of Main Street in Sayville, NY, except most of the restaurants there had outside dining. We ended up choosing this place called Blue Lagoon, or something with a blue. I don't remember exactly, but the name resonated with me. That is what really mattered. It had a very interesting menu, and to my stomach and hearts delight, I ate. I filled myself with pure goodness and nourished myself.

## Communion With

As you come to me
Divineness, intelligence surrounds me
The chambers are open, my chest expands
Ethereal cosmic love
His grace is upon me
His eyes, the windows of the soul
Our breathe quiet and still
Meditation occurs

# DAY #7 - MAY 16, 2010

Today, I have to say, all of the long days and many outings have gotten to me, although they were incredibly awesome and inspirational. I am thankful to say that through all of my travels, I have been able to eat pretty close to the diet that keeps my body functioning. I rested and took a nap, as my body really needed it. Besides, it was raining, and the temperature was actually around 65 degrees. I mean I was looking to get away from the cold in NY. How could this happen? It appears to me though that the temperature fluctuates in CA like a woman going through menopause. It could be scary. Be careful, and be prepared for anything. It was a good day for reading on crystal healing. Actually, since I have been recovering all of these months, that is what I do. Read, read and read. Feed the brain literally with knowledge. This afternoon, I had a masseuse come to the house I have been staying in, and it was quite interesting. It was a very interactive massage with a lot of breathing and manipulation. I enjoyed it very much but found later in the day that it was a bit much for my beautiful brain.

**C**ommunion (with)
**H**oly (ness)
**R**enunciation
**I**nitiation (into)
**S**acred
**T**emples

Through his words, he guides me to
get me closer to my true self

# DAY #8 - MAY 17, 2010

For the next two days, my brain was feeling mild to intermediate electrical shocks, which were very discomforting to me. The pain was high, and I had a hard time focusing. Honestly, I was very upset and spent some time crying, as it made me very nervous. This has never happened before. I think this particular type of massage was definitely not resonating with me.

Today is my father and youngest sister's BIRTHDAY. I am glad to be here resting, so it gives me the opportunity to spend more time with them in the future. I look forward to speaking with them.

### Mother

She awakens in the forest floor
Reviving creatures that have passed before
Her beauty is unspoken, and her words are like gold
Her presence is all that is needed to enliven your soul
Softly with the wind, she lulls out your name
You transcend into love, light then dissipate
All sorrows and pains are washed with the rains
Cleansed and complete mother awaits

# DAY #9 - MAY 18, 2010

I spent most of my day in bed not feeling well. The inflammation was severe and so was the pain. Please GOD, help me make it through. I do not really have much else to say except help. I often spend much time in bed (at least for the last 6 months) awake, but barely conscious. I remember so often, my daughters would be off to school early in the morning. I would try to wake and just be in their company, but I did not have the energy. It only felt like moments, but then they came home from school hours later, and I was just waking up.

I feel myself drift between worlds
My soul takes me to places, journeys I
cannot describe, but actually I can
Beautiful, surreal and peaceful
I feel the angels all around me calling my name
I lift my head towards the window
watching the clouds pass by
It all seems so far away
Will I wake for tomorrow?
Then I hear the words "Mom, are you okay?"

# Day #10 - May 19, 2010

I spoke with my children today. It was bitter sweet, as they were having some kind of discrepancy at home. The purpose of this trip was to avoid all stress, but apparently the adult in charge did not understand this. It was very difficult for me to leave my children for 30 days. I had to be selfish because I honor who I am. They are the only reason I have been strong all along.

You are what you feel…
So what are you?
Love, peace, joy, fear, anger, or sadness?
Feel what you are…

# Day #11 - May 20, 2010

I am still hearing the saga about my children. The key is to not give away your power to anyone. We keep our power in a loving nurturing way for ourselves. We deserve this. I mean, I did not think it was that big of a deal. It was not enough to stress me out, but, really, I was the one that allowed it. I certainly did that a lot when I was a teenager.

So much time passes by
Colors change, trees grow
Time to focus on the big picture
The plan that God has for me
Time to release all things that are not necessary
Focus on compassion and love
We all make mistakes
We learn, we grow
We heal

# DAY #12 - MAY 21, 2010

I am tired today and am spending my day reading inspiring books. I love Louise Hay, the author. She is such a wonderful being. I find her work uplifting when I am not feeling well or just in general. Thank you, Louise Hay, for gracing me with your insights and wisdom.

Put yourself first
For if you do not put your-self first
How can you truly be available to others?
Satisfy your true self by listening to your
inner voice, your body's reactions
Love yourself first, then others

# DAY #13 - MAY 22, 2010

I do not have much time left in CA. I am heading back tomorrow and wish I could stay longer. I am very thankful to the family that allowed me the space in their home to heal and recuperate. This was an act of kindness, and I truly express my gratitude.

> **A** being of light
> **N**othingness
> **G**oing beyond fear
> **E**nlightened souls
> **L**iving in the moment

# DAY #14 - MAY 23, 2010

Today was an early-to-rise kind of day. I had a flight to catch in the morning, and there was a lot of running around to do. I wanted to make sure I left the house in order, just like the way it was when I arrived. The flight went well. I think I slept most of it, which is always helpful. I was very fatigued by the end of the day, as there were layovers and such. This journey to California consisted of many planes, trains, and my brain. My next destination, for the remainder of my time, will be spent in Pennsylvania.

> To be aligned with oneself
> Outside influences inhibit you
> Understand your inner self
> Concentrate and focus
> Higher consciousness unites us all

# DAY #15 - MAY 24, 2010

I am getting adjusted to East Coast time again. I have to say, I do not do well with sleep deprivation. This is a major contributor to brain inflammation. It's not something I am very fond of. Not unless I enjoy the feeling of, for lack of a better description, when your skull feels like a walnut moving around in the shell. Did you ever hear that when you go to crack a walnut, and you hear and feel it moving around inside the shell? I know it's strange, but it is true. It is like having a draft in the back of your skull and all the cold air is coming through. For so many months, I would wear a scarf or some sort of hat or cap. This would assist in keeping the draft out. I did end up with quite a unique collection of caps though. This was a very uncomfortable time for me.

Temporary discomforts heighten my awareness
Breathe through it, in and out
I close my eyes and see you there
You hold me, I am warm, safe
My chariot awaits

# DAY #16 - MAY 25, 2010

I am now adjusting to my new living situation. Things are getting serious. I head for the kitchen, and it is not that impressive, but I will make it work for me. One thing I missed through my journeys in California was preparing my fresh wheatgrass and vegetable juices. Of course, there are many wonderful juice bars everywhere, but there is some kind of gratification when you do it yourself. We will see where this takes me.

At this point, I have been ingesting 8 ounces of fresh wheatgrass juice that I have been growing. That is quite a lot, I must say. I have been doing this all along, also with some assistance of friends and others. I was taking that amount for maybe six weeks, and then decreasing it, depending on my progress.

For those that are familiar with wheatgrass, at times, and it is very common, even with one ounce, to feel nausea and experience headaches. There have been many countless times where I have had to go running to the bathroom thinking I was going to vomit. This is all part of the detoxification process.

The stillness of my soul
The crackle of the fire fills me with
warmth deep within my tired bones
Each hair follicle moved from the wind as
the stillness turns my hair to leaves
My arms to branches, my legs to roots
I speak softly, kindly in an unheard language
No words exchanged or necessary
All that needs to be heard is heard
through the stillness of my soul
Mother I've longed for you – Oneness is complete

# DAY# 17 - MAY 26, 2010

Today I am soaking seeds for wheatgrass and sprouts, resting, and eating a lot of vegetables. I am excited about this. I learned so much from the teachings at the Ann Wigmore Institute in Puerto Rico. I cherish the time I had spent their. It has helped me to stay alive. Thank you so much, Ann Wigmore. You have been one of my angels. Of course, this could not be possible without all of the wonderful teachers at your institute.

Let there not be one day when the body is not in motion
Even if it may be only the raising of your arms

# DAY #18 - MAY 27, 2010

I have been tired. The change in the temperature is not serving me well. The sunshine and heat make me feel a lot better. There is not as much pain, or maybe I am just tolerating it better. I am going in and out of consciousness. My pillow and my stuffed animal, Pooh Bear, spend the day with me in bed. I find myself, like a child, finding comfort in this stuffed animal. I feel sad, and miss my children. I wish to hear their laughter. I want to go home.

I am a parent, child, and friend
What I wish for self and all other beings is
courage, strength, power, fearlessness, and love
You are what you allow yourself to become
Be a warrior

# DAY #19 - MAY 28, 2010

The good thing about being in Pennsylvania right now is that my older sister lives close by. She comes to spend time with me, and we go sit down by the Delaware River enjoying the sunshine whenever we can. The fascinating aspect about this river is its healing properties. It is good to be alone with her without the responsibilities of taking care of others. I am feeling more rested today and not in as much pain.

Lift up your heads
Communicate, look into each other's eyes
Let the words that roll off your tongue be of truth
Plant a seed within your self
Grow healthy
Grow strong

# DAY #20 - MAY 29, 2010

I talk to my children every couple of days. I really miss them. I am thankful for their support even though, sometimes, I wished they were more helpful. I imagine it is traumatic for teenagers to see their parent in such a condition that it makes them want to pull away just to protect themselves. Once I am rested, I look forward to spending time with them again.

I remember I would be so fatigued and tired. When they left for school, I would be in bed. Then they came home excited to see me, and they would find me still there, just waking up. It was sad.

I am that which I am
As you are I, I am you
Together we merge as one
United in body, mind, and spirit

# DAY #21 - MAY 30, 2010

Today, I am drinking a lot of green juices, but that is pretty typical for me. I have been fatigued again and find myself in need to rest more now than in the first half of my journey. I am having a hard time with others doing so much for me. It is time to let go of the ego mind and graciously allow whatever assistance I receive. It is okay to allow when it is needed.

As the shadows lurk
The thoughts
They flood your mind
Each cell stimulated
Upon the vibrations of your presence
Asking yourself which way is up?
Which way to the light?
Why am I going towards the light?
As the light encapsulates you the healing begins
Every ray resonating deep within
Cleanse and release between the layers
Breathing slowly, breathing deeply
Feel every cell, each sensation of energy
As if the rain was falling
From the heavens upon your skin
You open your eyes to see the light
She hovers above you singing joyfully
Trance-like and hypnotic
Her beauty is beyond words
You reach for her hand as the tears fall freely
You are home, you are everywhere
The stars, the sun, and the moon

# DAY #22 - JUNE 1, 2010

I was feeling emotional today. It feels like sometimes my body and my mind are not on the same page, incongruent with one another. I realized or really came to terms with the fact that since my last relapse, in March of 2010, some changes occurred. I am finally accepting that fact. Yes, sometimes I cannot remember certain things anymore. It's all good though because I know that I am really loved and supported. I was told that if I forgot certain things, my loved ones would make me a video so I could remember. I joked around and said, "Hey, there are always flash cards too!" It felt much better coming out into the open with this, I have to say.

## Avalon

A re-union with her
I lift my arms up towards the sky
She washes away my sin
Revealed and heard
"I am here again"
I am spoken of as I hear my name
My skin touches the leaves
I stand facing east pointing towards the stones
I circle to the west amongst the trees
I circle to the north facing the moon
I circle to the south towards the light
Voices whisper as I am passing by
Power circle speaks to me
The wind softly calls my name
I enter as I do, open hearted

# Day #23 - June 2, 2010

It was an active and productive day. We traveled to Long Island, NY, as that is where I had to get some testing done on myself. We decided to do all of the things that are not available in our area in Pennsylvania. I had fun, but wow, traffic always in Long Island. That I do not like. I was able to see a friend during and in between appointments. That worked out well and was very healing. Being in the presence of certain individuals just raises your frequency. Then it was off to lunch to my favorite restaurant out in Long Island, NY, called Salsa Salsa. It's a burrito bar, and I totally love it.

As I take the time to reflect
A lightness enters my heart and heaviness leaves my chest
I've traveled many roads giving and receiving what is necessary
Adapting to the flow of life
Adapting to the integration of my self

# Day #24 - June 3, 2010

After all that time out traveling yesterday, I am doing better than expected. I slept in late and ate well - mostly greens and super foods. The wheatgrass was exceptionally sweet today. There was a time where I just did not want to even have any more because I have been drinking so much of it for what seemed like forever. Just the smell of it caused some kind of deep emotional pain. It was just a reminder of the discomforts I was going through, but I worked through it. It is all a blessing.

## Magic

A magical space provided
Things grow lush and marvelous
Love radiating, surrounding me
You touch my skin
The water falls and trickles past my flesh
Breathing in peace, harmony
Your fingers pass over me softly
The moss covering the forest floor inviting all to come in
Come explore the possibilities
We chant incantations inviting the spirits to participate
We open our eyes to see kaleidoscope images
Butterflies, dragon flies, and so much more

# DAY #25 - JUNE 3, 2010

Today was a day of visiting people that have helped me heal and have stood by me in this journey of LIFE. I really enjoyed speaking with them, as it inspires me. I seemed pretty energetic by the time I came home, although it was late, 9:30 pm. I seem to be livelier today, and I really love that. I remember when I would wake up and did not feel like I ever slept. Sleep deprivation is what it is called. I definitely do not do well without sleep. It causes more inflammation, like I have mentioned before. Who would really enjoy that anyway?

One thing I have realized throughout this journey is that we must be mindful of who we keep company with. We should be aware of this, whether we are well or not. How many of us spend time with toxic people? How many of us feel drained because we keep company with individuals who drain us because we feel obligated? Sometimes it is best to love somebody from a distance. Besides, you have to take care of yourself first. This is not a selfish act but a selfless act. Your being deserves it.

## Silence

She walked by silently
No words were exchanged
Her lips tight and stiff
She carried her pain in her torso
Silence was her way
A ladybug landed on her shoulder
Her silence turned to laughter
Her lips soft and loving
Her golden eyes and darkened hair
with golden shimmers of light
Transformation occurred, and her body
moved in a continuous dance
Improvisational singing and exploration
to the dance of life

# Day #26 - June 4, 2010

I woke up at 7:00 am and felt very rested and energetic. I decided to clean around the house and do some gardening before my chiropractic appointment at 10:30 am. I really enjoyed hearing the birds in the morning and was thankful for the beautiful tree in the front yard that provides much shade. I had a green smoothie, along with a spoon of almond butter, before my appointment. Sounds like a perfect start to my day with nourishing foods of that nature. I really love the care and professionalism in this particular chiropractic office. They are very efficient and move you around from room to room, depending on what therapies you are receiving. I noticed, after several massages from different masseuses, that working on my head or close to it does not resonate with me. It leaves me with this kind of electrical shock on and off for one to two days. For the first time, today I told this particular massage therapist not to work near that area and to be very gentle on my neck, as to not stimulate my beautiful brain. She was very kind and received it well. It was an excellent hour, and I did not experience that discomfort at all.

Later in the day, I went to the creek over by Mott Street (this is where a pair of bald eagles reside up in the trees with their family). I had nice conversations there, and I felt at peace with myself and all living things. I went into the creek and did some standing asanas (yoga). To my surprise, the mother eagle was out of the nest and in my full view. Now this was a vision for all to see. It was as if GOD was saying, "Look at this! You took a leap of faith with your life. You are strong, and my EAGLE friend is watching you."

Being in nature is really healing. It is the best medicine and is always readily available. Please get yourself outside to hear the glorious sounds of the animals, insects, and trees. If you really listen, you will hear them. There is so much for us to learn from Mother Nature.

<u>Mott Street</u>

Calming
Energizing
Soothe my spirit
Feel me
Touch me
Free me
I am here
Sacred water, cleanse me
Sacred circle, take me
I am here
Feel me
Touch me
Free me
I am here

# DAY #27 - SATURDAY JUNE 5, 2010

I woke up today feeling a bit groggy. I'm not really sure why. I felt like I had some allergy symptoms. I showered and rinsed off with cold water to wake myself up, as today was very important for me. Today I was attending a workshop for different holistic modalities. It was very inspiring and enhanced the knowledge that I all ready carry within myself. Many teachers come into our lives. Some serve us better than others, but nonetheless, teachers they are. Something to acknowledge is that during our lifetime, we always carry the role of being both teacher and student. We just go through our life interchanging that role.

I am off to bed. It has been a very long, exciting, and somewhat draining day. I felt many emotions arise today, as it was deep and personal for me. There was much discussion about cancer. I never really allowed myself to give in to that, but sometimes it was hard. I did not want to give it any power. But today, the tears fell freely and quickly.

Today was also my nieces fourth birthday, and she is currently in Miami, Florida. I look forward to seeing her so I can surprise her with her gift and see her beautiful smile. To see such an innocent child is also very healing. They are still so in tune with their surroundings.

Settling, settling
The marrow in my bones
Penetrating my thoughts
The actions that I took
The damage that was done
Consequences that occur
Like a spirit in the night
Lost then found
Taking down the vacant sign
Claiming what is mine
My body is my own
Reunited once again
I am

# DAY #28 - JUNE 6, 2010

Again, I awaken feeling groggy and achy probably from all the sitting on Saturday. I think I am spending much time thinking of going home since my 30 days are almost up. It is not that I do not want to see my children or family. It is that I do not want to be surrounded by the drama of others, which is not good for my healing. I certainly miss my daughters though. I finally get myself motivated and have a green smoothie this morning. Then I head off for my one-hour walk with Marley (the most amazing four legged friend). A walk always soothes and calms my soul. The beautiful fresh air and quietness lulls me. I did some yoga down by the river today, and I was in peace with the universe. All was good. Before I head back home to NY, I stopped over at The Patisserie (a wonderful local bakery). I had some delicious herbal tea, and we shared a few almond biscotti and one chocolate-walnut biscotti. Amazing! This all took place on the front porch dining area. Sundays are quite peaceful, but sometimes can be active with the tourists in Milford, PA. I encourage anybody who is traveling this way to please stop at The Patisserie, as you will be delighted. That I can guarantee. I must have spent at least an hour and a half there. The breeze went through my hair, and the wind lifted my spirits. It is a lovely place to people watch also. I finally went back to my temporary living situation and continue with my dining. I developed an appetite, which is eating usually every two hours. Now I had fried eggs with some avocados. This seems to be my craving or desire lately, and it suffices my hunger. I realized, after much observation, that every couple of weeks, when I go through cravings for fried eggs, it is usually when I am starting to recover from a relapse. It has happened every time. I remember when I was barely eating anything a few months ago and about twelve pounds ago, all I wanted was fried eggs on tortillas with avocados. Honestly, aside from the cravings after recovering from brain swelling, what Colombian/Peruvian does not crave those things? It would be immoral of me.

Today, we received a disturbing call from a friend. It turns out his wife was just diagnosed with brain cancer, which really hit home for me. She told me it was bigger than a golf ball but smaller that a baseball. I, of course, offered whatever help I possibly could and supported them with whatever decision they chose to take regarding treatments. I had a hard time not thinking about it. I sent my blessings and prayers to her and her family. That is all I could do, and of course, just be a friend. After many hours had passed and evening set in, I spent much time on the front patio area having dinner and just listening to nothing. Isn't that awesome listening to nothing but just being? Later, we watched a movie, which is what we seem to do in the evening to relax just a little bit more.

Lights surround me
Encapsulated vortex of energy
Releasing impurities, letting go fears
Opening the gates to new possibilities
Reaching for your hand
Expanding your wings
I hear you
Songs of the wind
Energetic imprints
Love

# Day #29 - June 7, 2010

I am not even sure what to say about today except that I am really excited to go home and be with my family. I really missed them. This is the longest time I have spent away from them. I feel blessed and honored that I have had this opportunity to rest and get to see my children again. Death is not something to fear. It can actually be quite a peaceful experience if you allow yourself to let go.

I am always grateful for whatever amount of time God graces me with my children. How blessed am I to be able to hug them and look into their beautiful ocean eyes and to just hold them and not say anything. This is a gift for me. It truly is.

Beautiful child of my creation
Thank you for choosing me
Thank you for the love and compassion
You taught me well
I carried you in my womb
I nestled you in my bosom
You have given me strength
You are my light that shines
My constant inspiration with words of
encouragement and support
You beautiful old soul, thank you

# DAY #30 - JUNE 8, 2010

Today was a day full of mixed emotions. Without my wonderful supportive parents and children, this journey would not have been possible. I love you all dearly for all of your kindness and help when I was not well. Thank you, sister, for being there for me during phone conversations when I just needed somebody to listen to me. Also, for always telling me something funny during those phone conversations so I could get through the pain. Thank you so much to my friends and family members who engaged with me afterwards and understood why I had severed cords with them during this transition. You are all a blessing! You have all been wonderful teachers to me, and I express my deepest gratitude to you all. Most of all, thank you, GOD! You have given me the greatest gift of all - to continue in this physical body to accompany my children a while longer.

It is not the shadows to fear
Shadows are merely an opportunity to learn
Why is it here?
Why do you surround me?
What must I change within myself?
Choose your company wisely
They sometimes feed on your soul
Go deep within, into the darkness
Removing the layers
Light being that you are
You choose this path for growth
Do not forget your task
Remember your past
Use your tools
Soul being, find the way
You are awaited in the heavens

There are so many wonderful healing modalities that can assist one through their healing journey and transitions. Below is a list of some of the many modalities that the universe has provided for us. It is always encouraged to seek out a practitioner that one feels comfortable with. If you are not resonating with a particular modality or practitioner, it is your inner guide's way of saying that maybe this is not the way or the right time.

1. Acupuncture
2. Chiropractic
3. Color Healing
4. Energy Healing (Reiki and so many other forms)
5. Flower Essences
6. Gem/Crystal Therapy
7. Hydro-Colon Therapy
8. Massage
9. Meditation
10. Prayer
11. Raw Living Foods
12. Reflexology
13. Sound Therapy
14. Visualization
15. Yoga

# Inspirational Quotes:

"Never, never, never give up." Winston Churchill

"Life begins at the end of your comfort zone." Neale Donald Walsch

"Life isn't about finding yourself. Life is about creating yourself." Unknown

"There is a magic about you that is all your own." D.M. Dellinger

"Thank you for being." Seneca Greeting

"All growth is a leap in the dark." Henry Miller

"Be the change you wish to see in the world." Gandhi

"You can run, and you can hide, but you are everywhere you go." Malane Gargurevich

"It is easier for a camel to pass through the eye of a needle than for a rich man to enter the Kingdom of Heaven (Luke 18:25)." Jesus Christ

"Man's heart away from nature becomes hard." Standing Bear

"Health, contentment, and trust are your greatest possessions and freedom your greatest joy." Buddha

"When we learn to eat properly, we begin to rebuild our bodies and to fulfill our purpose on this planet: to grow in health, creativity, wisdom, and compassion." Dr. Ann Wigmore

"If you feel bound, you are bound. If you feel liberated, you are liberated. Things outside neither bind nor liberate you; only your attitude toward them does that." Sri Swami Satchidananda

"Everything should be as simple as it is, but not simpler." Albert Einstein

"Look deep into nature, and then you will understand everything better." Albert Einstein

"If you're going through hell, keep going." Winston Churchill

"Knowing others is intelligence; knowing yourself is true wisdom. Mastering others is strength; mastering yourself is true power." Lao Tzu

"Adopt the pace of nature, her secret is patience." Ralph Waldo Emerson

"If you change the way you look at things, the things you look at change." Wayne Dyer

"You alone are the judge of your worth, and your goal is to discover infinite worth in yourself, no matter what anyone else thinks." Deepak Chopra

"Believe you can, and you're halfway there." Theodore Roosevelt

# SUGGESTED READINGS:

1. "I Can Do It" by Louise Hay
2. "You Can Heal Your Life" by Louise Hay
3. "Heal Your Body" by Louise Hay
4. "Your Body Speaks Your Mind" by Deb Shapiro
5. "Angel Answers" by Diana Cooper
6. "The Wheatgrass Book" by Ann Wigmore
7. "Rebuild Your Health" by Ann Wigmore
8. "Wheatgrass Nature's Finest Medicine" by Steve Meyorwitz
9. "Living In The Raw" by Rose Lee Calabro
10. "Dowsing Beyond Duality" by David Ian Cowan and Erina Cowan
11. "The Way Of Herbs" by Michael Tierra
12. "Heal Your Life Home Remedies" by Hanna Kroeger
13. "Prescription For Nutritional Healing" by James F. Balch & Phyllis Balch
14. "The Healers Manual" by Ted Andrews
15. "Animal Speak" by Ted Andrews
16. "Flower Essence Repertory" by Patricia Kaminski & Richard Katz

17. "Communion with God" by Neale Donald Walsch
18. "Conversations With God Trilogy" by Neale Donald Walsch
19. "Autobiography Of A Yogi" by Paramahansa Yogananda
20. "The Holy Bible"

# Raw Living Foods

As said by Ann Wigmore, "Living foods are preferably organically-grown foods consumed in their original, uncooked state. Living Foods are prepared without cooking because cooking destroys the enzyme life force. The Living Foods Lifestyle® is vegan. It uses no meat, dairy, or any other animal product.

However, Living Foods are not simply raw foods. Because many people cannot digest raw foods, Living Foods are prepared in a way that makes them easy for the body to assimilate and extract optimal nourishment. Living Foods include young greens, such as sprouted nuts, seeds, and grains; cultured preparations; and dehydrated foods. Fresh wheatgrass juice adds an unparalleled level of nutrition, vitality, and health."

Raw Living Food Recipes:

These are some of my favorite. Get creative and make your own. There are many wonderful books out there as well.

1.  Sprouted Trail Mix:
    ½ C hemp seed
    ½ C raisins
    1 C sunflower seeds
    1C pumpkin seeds
    ½ C almonds
    ¾ C apples of your choice

    Please note this applies to sunflower, pumpkin, and almonds (soaked, drained & dehydrated at 95 over night or 8 hours). Apples are diced into small pieces & dehydrated along with the seeds and nuts. Apples may or may not take longer to dehydrate. Use your judgment. Mix everything together and store in a tightly-sealed glass jar. It will last a couple of weeks.

2.  Mango Madness Smoothie:
    ½ C banana
    ½ C mango
    2 large carrots
    2 Tbs. coconut butter
    ¼ C soaked walnuts (drained)
    2 C water
    ½ -1 C ice cubes

    Put all ingredients in the blender. Blend and enjoy.

3. Green Machine Smoothie:
   5 kale leaves
   3 pears
   3-4 C water
   3 Tbs. hemp
   ¼ C soaked almonds (drained and peeled)

   Put all ingredients in the blender. Blend and enjoy.

4. Spirulina Smoothie:
   1 Tsp. of spirulina
   3 Tbs. raw nut butter
   1 large frozen banana
   1 C ice cubes
   1 C nut milk

   Put all ingredients in the blender. Blend and enjoy.

5. Nut Milk:
   1 C soaked nuts (almonds or Brazil nuts)
   3 C water
   1 Tsp. salt

   *If using almonds, you must blanch them and peel off skin. Put all ingredients in the blender and let whip for a few minutes. Then strain the liquid through a nut milk bag, which separates the liquid from the nut meal. Nut meal can be dehydrated and used as flour for another recipe.

6. Brazil Nut Macaroon:
   2 C Brazil nut meal (or other nut meal)
   3 C coconut (shredded)
   2 Tbs. vanilla
   ¾ C maple syrup

   Mix all ingredients together very well in a glass or stainless steel bowl. Form into balls or desired shape or you may use tablespoon measuring spoon for precise measurement. Dehydrate for 18 hours at 105.

7. Dehydrated Plantain Pinwheels:
   2 large ripe plantains
   ½ Tsp. sea salt
   2 Tsp. oregano
   2 handfuls of fresh cilantro
   ½ C water

   Put all ingredients in the blender. Puree to a cream. Then spread on a teflex sheet and dehydrate at 95 overnight (about 8 hours). In the morning, peel off of teflex sheet and flip pinwheels over. Dehydrate for 3 - 4 hours. You can stuff pinwheels with avocado or fresh slivers of mango.

8. Dehydrated Flatbread:
   1 ½ C sprouted wheat berries
   1/3 C flax seeds (soaked)
   1 Tbs. chia seeds
   1 Tbs. hemp
   1 large banana
   1 C water

Put all ingredients in the blender. Blend well, but you want to leave this a bit more on the grainy side. I use 1/3 of a cup for each flat bread. Spread on a teflex sheet to desired shape (square or circular). Dehydrate at 95 overnight (about 8 hours). In the morning, peel off of teflex sheet, flip over, and dehydrate 3-4 more hours. Use flat bread with any spreads of your liking (jam, butter, etc.).

*Please note that with any dehydrated food, especially in large quantities, one must increase their intake of liquids, preferably water. Also note when using almonds, after soaking and rinsing you should peel of skin by either blanching in warm water or room temperature water.

**Complimentary Modality – Working with the Chakras Using Colors, Sounds, and Crystals**

| Chakras | Color | Sound | Crystal |
|---|---|---|---|
| 1. Root Chakra | Red | Lam | Garnet |
| 2. Sacral Chakra | Orange | Vam | Moonstone |
| 3. Solar Plexus | Yellow | Ram | Tigers Eye |
| 4. Heart Chakra | Green | Yam | Malachite |
| 5. Throat Chakra | Blue | Ham | Lapis Lazuli |
| 6. Brow Chakra | Indigo | Om (Aum) | Amethyst |
| 7. Crown Chakra | Violet | Om (Aum) | Clear Quartz |

# Epilogue

As we are now entering the year of 2014, much time has passed since the beginning of writing this book. I was plagued for much time in between these time frames, but in the now, I feel wonderful and renewed. I experienced many transitions and life changes that are unimaginable, but with the grace of God, Creator, Spirit, and all of his or her assistants, I am here and well.

Though many months at a time were spent in bed, I was always divinely guided on what process or step I should take next during my meditations, such as which healers or modalities I would benefit from at that particular point in time. This applied even as to what prayers to read. Different angelic beings presented themselves to me, along with deceased loved ones, guiding me along the way. How blessed was I and my family for such assistance.

My family and I have grown stronger through this experience. It was all very real for us, and our bond now is quite unique. We, my children and I, are all very aware of what surrounds us in this physical and non-physical world. The knowing that we have for one another is tremendous, and this is something that I cherish deeply.

I now reside in a rural area of Pennsylvania. I am deeply committed to Mother Nature and spend much time outdoors. Being in the woods is part of my medicine. My connection with her (Mother Nature) is a very deep relationship, and if I do not spend much time outdoors, I start to feel like a fish out of water. She sustains me. There is much conversation that takes place in the woods with plant and tree beings and many others. I often find myself in conversations with them, and what a delight it is.

I am very in tune now with energetic vibrations within myself and my surroundings at all times. With that being said, I have come to know that there are particular stressors to avoid as to not cause any disharmony within my precious, delicate brain or in my field, in general. I focus on the power of intention and surround myself with love. I choose to radiate and receive love at all times, giving and receiving. We still are human, and sometimes we may fall, but simply get yourself back up and shine to the heavens.

Today, in the now, I focus on awareness. I choose to be aware of all things, especially thoughts. Aware of cause and effect, for every action there is a reaction. I choose to leave you with that message. Be aware of your surroundings, and be kind to yourself. We are but gentle creatures, and we all have a purpose. My purpose was to learn through this disharmonious state that took place to assist others. And through cosmic law, everything happens for a reason. Past actions (karma) come into our present time for growth and to finish up what we have started.

I share these beautiful words as they were channeled during my stay in Quito, Ecuador, from God to you.

I am with you at all times, through times of darkness when your thoughts are dimmest. Be reassured "I AM" with you at all times. Align yourself. Close your eyes. Take a breath. Can you see me?

It is not the fear that constricts you. It is the unnecessary repeated patterns that cause illness to the physical being. What is it that holds you from moving forward? Every cell carries a vibration. If your vibration is of a lower frequency due to emotional, mental, physical, or spiritual stagnation, it will not serve you well.

You are the white light that shines into the heavens. We are all One. My goal, or my desired outcome, is to encourage you to gracefully move forward to the light. As we rise together into the heavens, our souls re-unite.

Angels, Mother-Father, God, we are here to guide and direct you, as we are here to serve you in love.

There is a space within myself. It holds the torch. Forgiveness is granted, and all is forgiven. My heart mends. There is peace, joy, and clarity. There is light, an open beacon. Can you not see it shine upon you?

Emotions (out of balance) = Disharmony

Connectedness, Communication, and Continuation = Transformation

One journey ends, and another journey begins. They blend into one another as transformation occurs. Be well, and be true to yourself. Listen to your heart open and expand. Your heart consciousness will assist with connecting you with the higher consciousness that is available to all. I love you.

These moments that are still
These moments that are quiet
One listens intently to the heart's desire
In this stillness, expansion occurs
I open myself to you Spirit
I am yours for the taking
We breathe as One
The elixir of life
Fresh morning dew
Cover my skin with your sweet grass
Bathe my soul with your subtleness
Your roots at the heels of my feet
Walk with me gently, as we sing with the sounds of the wind

Darkness covers
Fire spirits
Deep enchantments of our soul
Keep them coming, there's no surprise
Grandfather always knows
Keeper of the darkness
Keeper of the fire
Light the way and set us free
Purification
Revelations
Chanting
Drumming
Set us free
Mother Earth
Father Sky

Silence stirs
Open eyes
Purple crystal goddess
Do as you will
Consciousness
Expansion
Particles
Light
Trans-form
Whole-ness
Goddess wings of golden sun
Raise me high forevermore

# WORDS FROM MY BELOVED FATHER:

Do not let my death sadden you. I did not die. I just changed form. I am everywhere.

At this time, all is linear. Time does not exist. So in this moment, I am here with you always. I am not to be forgotten by you, but remembered in a way that lifts you up, support you through your own transformation, and this is why you chose me to be your father. I love you.

Death is an illusion. Humans place it in a category under parameters. Death is a gift when you can embrace it lovingly and consciously. This I thank you for, my child. You supported me during this next adventure of my life and stood by me from the beginning to the end, no matter what. I know this was difficult and made many others uncomfortable. You honored me, and I am thankful.

I wish for all of you to be well. This is a time to rejoice and celebrate. I am free, and I am home. I was unhappy. I carried so much, and my soul was ready. Forgive me. I love you.

I was afraid. I didn't want to let go, but I was tired also. I didn't want my family (all of you) to see me suffer. I felt embarrassed. That was my main concern. I realized how much love you had for me, that you were always there by my side and placed this cocoon-like energy around me. It made me feel free. I am not sure how to explain it. I once said during this state, "Is this confusion or communion?" Perhaps, at first, you were confused to hear me say such a thing, and so was I, but you later understood what I meant. Dying was a communion, as I was guided towards this light all the time. I wanted to go home. This also brought confusion to some family members. I wanted to go home. I wanted to be with my Eternal Father. Many of my loved ones passed before me, and I never let that go. It was painful. Please, what I would like to share is that you try and not hold onto things for so long. To try and fix things right away, to ease your suffering, or not have any at all. I had a hard time with change, and this was very noticeable to my family. Change is important. I just didn't like it.

Let go. Let go of mourning. Live your life

# RE-UNION WITH MY FATHER:

I close this book with these paragraphs, as they were expressed to me during waking or sleeping state with my father".

It was one week since Daddy had passed, and he and I had our first reunion. There were two black cars, one parked in front of the other. We were parked on a dirt road on acres of a beautiful green field. I was the driver of my vehicle and was sitting in my car during the visit, while dad stood outside of his vehicle on the passenger side. Dad seemed to have a chauffeur (GOD), and they were parked in front of me. He had this beautiful cat rubbing and purring at his feet, and they both seemed very happy. My father was radiant, glowing, looked healthy, and was smiling. Our conversation began. I said, "Dad, why don't you take the cat with you?" He looked at me so lovingly with a big smile and said, "I can't. I am going to Florida." It was that simple.

NOTE: The cat in this dream appeared to my daughters and I when we first started caring for my father. He was homeless and undernourished and showed up at our door. I never expected to keep him, but as dad said in a later visit during one of my visions, "He's a gift." He was here to comfort us during our loss. A few months passed, and I'd been on many road trips. I spent some time in Florida in solitude exploring. Then it dawned on me that my father's best friend lived there. I was supposed to be leaving the following morning, but I changed my flight and drove seven hours to connect with his best friend. This is the one that he was visiting when he said he was going to Florida. It also dawned on me that the rental car I had in Florida was the same one in my dream. It was all coming together. While driving to St. Augustine to see my father's friend, my dad and I had many conversations. It was very touching and beautiful and I shed many a tear. When I finally arrived at his friend's home, I passed along the message that my dad wanted me to relay, "I want you to know I just drove seven hours just to give you a hug." Dad liked to joke around a lot and bust chops. His friend was a bit shocked and emotional. He began to cry. His friend mentioned that a few days prior to dad's passing, and several times after, that dad had visited him and his wife, pretty often actually. They had felt his spiritual presence. This journey was completely spontaneous and intuitively guided. There was no concern or hesitation on my part as to what if I drive seven hours and he's not there. I trusted the guidance, and his friend and I were able to meet and had beautiful conversations regarding my father. I felt honored to carry out this task that I had been unexpectedly given. Thank you again, Daddy. I love you.

In a dream, I extended my right hand and dad his left unto mine. I felt his fingers. He reached out to hug me, as I burst into tears. I felt him as the last time we hugged before he became ill. I saw him in the coat he liked to wear and standing by the kitchen in his apartment. The energy from his presence was warm and tingly. A sensation that brought joy, as the tears fell. This was a tremendous loss in this realm, but we were very thankful for the merging of all realms, as it allows us to connect in this way.

Today, during a healing session, as I called him, Dad came into my field while I was treating his granddaughter. He held her right hand, and then kissed her on the forehead. He said I love you. Then he kissed her again on the forehead, released her hand, and walked off into nothingness.

In my dream state, dad came to me. I had just recently moved, actually within days. In this dream I had a few relatives helping. My nephew took this object off of the wall, passed it to his wife, Kristine, who then passed it to my father. My dad held this large object up in the air and walked right in front of me (several times). I was so happy to see him. I shouted excitedly, "Dad you're here," but he just kept walking. I said this several times, and I was wondering why he was ignoring me. He continued to walk out the door of my home. I followed him, but then I lost him, and I became completely lost. I did not know how to get home, and I felt confused. In essence the message that came through was, "Don't get so caught up in trying to find me. I will just come to you." Do not lose yourself in this process, it just comes naturally.

All these experiences were very dear and personal to me, it touched me in a way that is indescribable, but yet it is. Like a soft warm light on your skin that soothes you.

Printed in the United States
By Bookmasters